ESSEX CLAY

# Essex Clay

ANDREW MOTION

FABER & FABER

First published in 2018
by Faber & Faber Ltd
Bloomsbury House
74–77 Great Russell Street
London WC1B 3DA

Typeset by Hamish Ironside
Printed in the UK by Bell & Bain Ltd, Glasgow

A CIP record for this book is available from the British Library

ISBN 978-0-571-33996-9

10  9  8  7  6  5  4  3  2  1

*Gillian Motion 1928–1978*
*and*
*Richard Motion 1921–2006*

# Acknowledgements

Acknowledgements and thanks are due to *The Echo Chamber* (BBC Radio 4), on which a part of this poem was broadcast in December 2017.

# Contents

# ESSEX CLAY

# PART ONE

The intact frost of early morning
and a blade of ice
drawn from the tap in the stable yard.

The village as they drive through
half asleep under twisting chimneys.

The church     Victorian Doomsday
moored to the hilltop edge
with its pretty flotilla of graves.

The weathervane cockerel's gold and flying eye.

The lane
straightening beside water meadows
under a thatch of bare chestnuts
shattered with daylight.

Gravel in the ford
washed by the brimming stream
the Blackwater
and pebbles magnified     tawny     beach colours
with that other river     the river of shining tar
shivering underneath.

Last night's snowdust
in suddenly wide-open ploughed fields.

Flints like hip bones and knee bones.

Clay clods supporting
miniature drift-triangles on their windward side.

His mother silent beside him
        her yellow hair trapped and placid in a hairnet

her clean cream jodhpurs   red collar   black riding jacket

    her stock like a bandage

        her gold pin
                adorned with the mask of a fox.


                    *


He is seventeen      confident      opinionated
                and definitely at odds
                            on this subject at least.

        He does not approve.

    But     when he glances into the footwell
and sees his mother's narrow feet
                fluffy sheepskin slippers
            paddling by turns at the brake
                    accelerator      clutch
        he is silent.

He cannot bring himself
                to have that argument again.


                    *


    In the car park of the White Hart
                also the bus stop
he reminds himself

no one makes a scene        not at his age

and condescends             tips his head a little
      to kiss his mother goodbye.

A skim of skin
      is enough.

But he does see and cannot forget her hairnet in close-up
      a black cobweb        tougher of course

      and feels it
            scratch
                  the tip of his nose.

Then he is out in the wind buttoning his overcoat
      the ankle-length        topsoil-brown        itchy
            war-time soldier's greatcoat
                  the British Warm
                        borrowed from his father's wardrobe
      without permission
                  stolen actually
which makes him        beside his holdall
            a soldier himself
                  he imagines.

*

Exactly as his mother grinds the Hillman back into gear
      the silhouette of his bus
            bulges over the hilltop beyond the White Hart.

He flinches away
      to discover his mother's face is

already no longer her face
but an after-image
hovering a little way behind her
as she guns the engine      and wriggles into
the traffic flow.

Her exhaust plume rapidly fades into the spectre of
a spectre.

Dark petrol-dribbles escaping the pipe
might well be a trail of crumbs
dot-dot-dot all the way home.

*

The bus is almost past him now      except
when he hoists his arm
the whole snow-filthy bulk amazingly

stops.

Double doors hiss open.

Cigarette fug flops out.

And in he steps
with too many hands
or not enough hands
to pay the fare
to manage the bloody holdall
to hold                         tight.

It's OK sonny it's OK.

Twirling up to the top deck
        stumbling as the bus surges and sashays
            forward
                with a shudder through every one of its
                    body plates
he lurches for a last glimpse of the lane back to the
    village
        and finds no car in sight.


                            *


From this height
        smearing the window mist with his sleeve
            the whiskery sleeve that makes an O
        fringed with delicate nettle-hair scratch marks
he can see across a whole cabbage field
        creased with snow.

            And no one the entire journey
        to notice even        let alone ridicule
                either the relief
                    or the alarm of solitude
he reveals by leaning his head against the glass
                on the trembling chill
        and pretending he is asleep.

Although                    despite appearances
        he is still watching in fact        vaguely
the shadow of the bus shrink
        where it meets a burst of heavy snow
            then elongate as the snow weakens

so one minute he sees himself not at all
    the next topples forward across hedgerows
    brick walls
        window panes
            cars shawled at the curbside
                shop fronts        mannequins
                    slopes of threadbare winter wheat

and below this the clay six feet deep
        malevolent pasty face
            ash smears and ochre
a dead weight but in fact alive
    sluggishly
        waiting with all the time in the world
to sculpt its lead around gumboots and plough blades
            to rear and obliterate whatever it can

until an hour has gone and the bus flusters
    into Sawbridgeworth
        where its shadow abruptly
falls in through the windows and sinks down
        among the other shadows already assembled
            and is absorbed.

                        *


Clambering out
            holdall thumping the door
he forgets himself
        the instant he sets eyes upon her.

Juliet.

    Her face and love-name coinciding.

Her black hair      black
        not a black enough word.

        Her red mouth.

    Her skin white      but mainly full
        ripeness.

And she is looking straight at him.

    She is.

        Glittering and
    ignoring her fluttery mother beside her
which he should not.

    He shakes her mother's hand
headscarf      specs      face-fuzz powder.

    But for Juliet

            their cheeks brush-collide
and he smells
            mint.

    Should have thought of that.

Never mind.
            Just find the car
                boot tricky
                crammed already
with a clutch of decapitated shopping-bag fledglings.

    It's OK sonny it's OK.

Then next question.

Front seat or back.

Back.

But hunching forward        laying one forearm flat
    on pale-green clammy plastic
Juliet's black hair a swelling wave
     trapped inside her collar
      until they set off

        and the heater cranks up

and Juliet
     slips her hand
    inside this wave of black to set it free
     and it flood-slithers
over the shoulders of her coat onto his hand
     which jolts in the electric shock.

       *

Afternoon      already      somehow
and Juliet's mother has disappeared thank you God
    she has work to do
  while     despite the cold
the clouds and snow flurries
    shovelling west from Siberia
      he and Juliet leave the house for a walk.

He spares a thought for his own mother.

Will she be home already
                defeated
she would say that
                defeated
                        by cold.


Her voice stays with him through the back yard
        ghosting


                        boiler shed
ghosting
                        dog kennel
ghosting
                        wood shed
ghosting.


        But he cannot hear what the ghost says.



                        *



They step from the lee of the house
                immediately into ice puffs
where cold slits his eyes


        and he sees ahead            guesses rather
a dead prairie sprinkled with snowstones
                his greatcoat
                        not so ridiculous now


        no more than Juliet's white fur hat and
Afghan or            Doctor Zhivago number
        fur blustering at collar and wrists
                while she butts into the wind

arms folded tight      hugging herself
one blue vein pulsing in her porcelain neck.

\*

As for his own face
    he cannot      dare not
  what with eyes streaming     whole face
stiff like a stroke    but still
    blathering       this and that
        this and that
    their destination of all things
next year's Christmas trees
      dimly darkening the horizon.

\*

Well
      they do ask for it farmers
    ripping everything out
  hedges      hundreds of years
    shelter.

\*

And yet he still does manage
to lead her on.

As she leads him
down the long narrow headland

snowflakes glued on the winter wheat shoots
            dithering beside them.


                        *


Jesus though
        laughable this cold
            laughable and
suddenly it gets the better of him.

So he veers
            leaf blown
                    back the way they came.

But Juliet is deliberately standing in his way.

                And his mouth
        did she mean this
            obviously she meant this
                his mouth
blurs runnily back to life in the warmth of her mouth.

            For a moment there is

    pure darkness.

        Pure slippery deepening wet dark.

            And heat
    as his hand slides inside her coat.

Astounding radiator heat.

When he touches bare skin
        between the waist of her jeans and her jersey
and Juliet slides her mouth from his mouth to his ear
        where she pours into him
                the blaze of his own name.


                        *


                He wants her now.

He wants her
        among the snowdropped wheat tips
and flints
        gleaming between the seed drills.

        In the slicing snow swipes.

Under the weightless silk cloud sheet.

                A perfectly ridiculous idea.

Although
        when they bow towards the house
                arms looping each other's shoulders
against the wind opposing
        they realise    what they have promised each other.


                        *


There is an hour before they must change
                                for the party.

Juliet insists
              they have to go.


    After she has dragged the curtains shut
after she has lit the fire
        after she has flicked through her box of LPs and
            chosen
                *Music from Big Pink*


                  soul mate


        he stands to one side of the room by the curtains
              a proper     young     man
beside the floor-length wall-to-wall expensive blue
    velvet curtains
              with snow falling outside
                  and agrees.


              Of course they must.


        He stares flagrantly at her in the armchair
              to show he would rather not.


    Knees drawn up     legs curled round like
          a mermaid on a rock


        not that


                  like herself
                  right hand shielding her eyes
        concentrating on 'The Weight'
                    *I pulled in to Nazareth*
    left hand     square-tipped fingers

tightening round her bare ankle
and the little vein mesh there
the blood delta
pale lavender.

*

When he has made his point
he collects and removes himself to the spare room
as ordered
the soft-lit     oak-panelled
low-ceilinged spare room.

Here he prepares himself.

He takes time
shaking out creases
from his new white shirt with the jabot collar.

He sounds     with all he dares of his weight
the nervous springs in the high bed.

He begins to imagine

or will it be her room.

*

A knock
the polite wood-knuckle sort.

Juliet.

Has she          what
          has she
     changed her mind.

     Is it now.

Then the door creaks and
          he sees not Juliet
Juliet's mother
     and the look of her makes his smile
               stiffen.

He thinks
                    is she
     peering into his head.

     Is she          about to forbid.

But that would not explain why
          she is crying.

     It would not explain why
          she is wiping tears from both eyes
pinching her nose as if she might sneeze
     dimpling the eiderdown with her fingertips
               the silvery blue eiderdown
               stitched into lumpy waves
to occupy herself with the patterns she makes.

               *

     A grown woman
          talking as she is crying.

Like suffocation.

But she does say clearly enough
methodical for a moment at least
his father has called on the telephone.

His father has called
and his father.

He interrupts.

With the inspiration of dread
a mind-burst
like a sapling
twigs        branches        quick green flickering
instantly becoming a tree
he tells her        he already knows
what she has to say.

And true
there is nothing like surprise in his voice.

Brain juddering.

Turbulence.

But even that soon settles down
the air he breathes becoming perfectly smooth and
steady again
and him dry-eyed

at one remove from himself admittedly
watching himself
as Juliet's mother tells him

squinting at her watch
      restraining the frilly white cuff of her blouse

his mother now
      just exactly now in fact
         as they are speaking

his mother is in surgery because

      she is still not looking at him
      she is still studying her watch

his mother is in surgery at St John's Hospital in
  Chelmsford
      where his father has already arrived.

Because of the accident      he tells her impatiently
      and wants to add
         but does not add
      takes pity on her
         as she backs away to the door
      both hands covering her mouth
adds to himself at least

      he has expected this all his life
feared would be better
      he has feared this all his life
and the only surprising thing
      but he cannot say this
      the only surprising thing is

      he wants to know more than anything
         where Juliet is
the corridor      her room      waiting

not waiting any more
　　　　　how could she be
　　　　　　waiting
or him
　　　how could he wait for her
　　　　　　after this.

　　　　　　　*

But they do go to the party.

　　　　　　It is explained
　　　　he cannot return home
there is no one

　　　　　　and his father
　　　Juliet's mother says
　　　　　　his father thinks the party will stop him

　　　what

worrying.

　　　　　He doubts very much
　　　　　　worrying is the word
　　　and that
　　　　　is another thing he will not say.

Instead
　　　he will do as his father wants.

He will     because of this
        seizing the new word     new to him
             injury.


         *


    He tries it again under his breath
        injury
when Juliet's mother ushers him
        injury
and Juliet out of her car at the party
        then spins away
             in a red-flare exhaust-ghost snow-flap

        relieved
        he understands

while he and Juliet
        not escaping the icy lunge
             of a magnolia hand by the front door
        injury
so he is soaked along the left arm of his new white shirt
        the shirt his father hates

while he and Juliet
        duck into this stranger's house
    he thinks might not even exist
except as a stack of crammed and shining rooms
    bolted together with injury
        with bars of very loud music.


         *

In the emptied-out dance room

empty apart from the Stonehenge sideboard
    which will never be the same again
        after that fag-end gouging a ruby furrow

in the space-trip spangling disco ball light

    in the profound heat
        and rock-thrash

he must tell everyone
        he has this new distinction
    at the top of his lungs if necessary.

His mother is dying        probably
        even as he stands here.

    His mother is dying.

But the room        the entire house
    decides this is not important
        and the music drowns it.

The music        the dancing
    the talk of nothing
        of everything but.

Juliet will not have it either.

    She is under orders
    and motherly a bit.

He must be cheerful
he must be occupied
he must be distracted.

So

    here she is now     refilling his drink
    here she is now     introducing him
    here she is now  mouthing his name
    here she is now  finding a side room
    and settling herself     onto his knee
    on both knees now     in his lap
    with her    slippery weight and heat
    moulding him through the dusk-red
    satin trousers she has made herself

and

              in the run-up to midnight
     after someone has dimmed the lights

in the maze of a slow song

    fatuous lyrics    he can hear that    fatuous
        but who cares

    laying her long bare arms on his shoulders
        allowing him to breathe
the sleepy vanilla scent in the crease of her elbows
     linking her fingers behind his neck
        resting her forehead on his forehead
        her black hair
           her skin sealed to his skin

as if her thoughts could fill him
       as if she could flood him
with the perfect blank of her superior happiness.


*


It is embarrassing
            or something
when they slither into the deep cracked back seat
       of her mother's Rover
because at midnight sharp she has come to collect them.

He wishes the meat of his neck and shoulders
       were bruised by the weight of Juliet's arms.

He wishes his whole body had scorched
       when she nested on his knees
              in her sleek satin.

He wishes his mind had received her mind
       like a lake swallowing the stream that feeds it.

He wishes.

            And yet.

Although they are leaning together holding hands
       welded in the sublunary capsule of the car
he discovers after a mile or two
       Juliet is not noticeable to him.

       Not really.

Not compared to the silence
      hardening between the three of them
as witch trees weave their way home into a tunnel.

Not compared to the doubly darkened air
      sharpening polar blue dots
          and pin-prick foxy eyes
in the fuel gauge and speedometer.

Not compared to Juliet's mother sparking a cigarette
      then milling open her window
          the smoke tugged outside
              like a streak of chalk
while at the same time
      allowing shavings of the night flying past them

to curl in
      pure          sharp

despite the blurry cigarette whiff
      which he discovers
gives him a feeling of drowning
      of sinking below the frozen surface of the world
but also of rising
      of becoming a ghost himself

until     when he turns his head
      now ignoring Juliet entirely
he sees in the tunnel of the lane behind them
      in the tail lights
where gravel flares under the narrowing branches

a wreckage trail
        made of his mother's possessions
    her riding jacket      her red collar
    her jodhpurs           her sheepskin slippers
    her Teasmade           her *Ring of Bright Water*
    her pair of pretend tortoiseshell hairbrushes
                and mirror
        her stock      her gold pin with the fox mask
    her black velvet hard hat
her whole wardrobe of everything in fact
        not much for a life
vanishing along with the moment he sees it
            as the pasty clay hand stretches
from underground and grabs.

                        *

The Rover whooshes in
    between what must once have been gateposts
the gate itself long gone
        as Juliet's mother flicks her cigarette
out through the window crack
            and winds the handle backwards.

The cold stops at once.

The snow
        slows down.

The snowflakes in the headlights
    cleverly assemble
        into a swivelling cone
            centred exactly on him.

He deliberately resists
    their attempt at hypnosis.

He sees the cigarette bounce once on the gravel
    fizz
        and shrink to a glowering red eye
            that keeps watching.

*

When Juliet's mother has parked her car in the garage

when he has climbed out
    into the rank petrol stink
        the suicidal exhaust fumes

when he has negotiated
    the child's sleigh        spare tyre
      Flit spray    garden hose
festooning the walls

when they have slithered in from the snow blast
    to the shimmering kitchen

Juliet's mother reminds him he must be tired
    recommends Juliet to fetch him a glass of water
        and tramps upstairs
thinking she is doing him and Juliet a favour.

Her door eases shut at the far end
    of the long brown top-landing carpet with a sober
    click
        and he thinks no more about her.

He thinks almost nothing.

He has no room for anything.

He notices            instead.

He notices

from the wicker dog basket
        creaks
as the dog      they have hardly been introduced
    a black Labrador
                sidles in from the hallway
        rotates once
and flops

        clock ticks
            from the moronic moon face
                    beaming above the Aga

    house plant
            aspidistra is it      keep that
flying then
            stiff green flag shreds

    water
            the glass Juliet has brought him
misting on the kitchen table
        while he rubs the side of his thumb to and fro
            across the hysterical woodgrain
years of scrubbing have exposed as ridges

    Juliet
            leaning the small of her back against the sink
head down      face streaked by hair fallen forward again

shoes off
        stretching her toes.

This silence     he thinks
        this silence
but he cannot complete the thought.

    A minute later
he drinks a mouthful of the water.

Another minute
    he says good night and retreats upstairs.

\*

The moon peers at him
    over her neat cloud fold
and decides       it is time to change her orbit.

    She swings closer to the Earth.

    She whispers to him
in a white voice like ice fixing grass
    that now she has taken over the duties of the sun.

        That her bright light
            will shine by day
as well as by night.

    And he accepts this.

He turns his face upwards
    and spreads his arms as wide as possible.

The moon in sympathy
        rests her entire weight
    on the shell of his chest.

He embraces her and
        she absorbs him.

                He feels nothing at all.

                *


Next morning the bus station is deserted.

    In the front seat of Juliet's mother's car he waits.

He asks himself
    what does the back of his head look like
            to Juliet behind him
    and has no idea.

            He waits.

He breathes on the windscreen
        until gradually        patchily
    the mist tide retreats.

            He waits.

He thinks the concrete walls of the bus station sparkle
    or is that his imagination.

            He waits.

Certainly in his imagination
    he sees the Earth dangling
clear in the frost of its fatal winter
      in its epic and eternal lack of deliberate intent
      its brainless habit     not even habit
condition
    its condition of perpetual accident.

        He waits.

And when his bus eventually fusses into the station
      under the almost-too-low dry-blood-coloured steel
        girder
and other passengers materialise from the supermarket
   adjacent
      and from High Street patting snow off their over-
       coats
        he makes his goodbye.

       Not a kiss

    an embrace sort of for Juliet
       twisting over the seat dividing them

and for her mother a handshake
    which she rejects
briskly negotiating the steering wheel
    to smother then fling him away
      bundling his holdall after.

The car door behind him slams shut
    as the double door of the bus

      opens.

He steps towards it        the exact fare ready in his fist
   and the collar of his army greatcoat up round his
      ears
         tickling a bit.


   No need to show that.


Keep going
      OK.


      Pay
         OK.


         Turn OK
            and wave.



                *        *        *

In the car park of the White Hart
a neighbour     Mrs Hill     is waiting for him
    boxy in her boxy Land Rover.

He is thinking     if he is thinking
    the same as yesterday.

    Snow on the wind.

Glittering gravel glued together by frost.

The pub sign
    wincing in its frame.

Wham     wham     wham
    shuddering past on the A120.

Even the darker skewed tyre tracks
    carved by his mother's Hillman
        still present and correct.

At least Mrs Hill does not ask him
    how was the party.
            She avoids that pothole.

    Also     she has no idea about Juliet
and he will not say.

However     what can she tell him about his mother.

As Mrs Hill twists the ignition key
    hunches over the steering wheel
        and they kangaroo forward

she manages     mostly
    to keep control of the matter-of-fact voice
        she has evidently rehearsed all morning.

His father has rung to tell her
what the others had told him
since he himself saw nothing.

His mother's pony Serenade
was jumping out of a copse.

She pecked. His mother fell.

She injured      she injured
her head        and she lay
unconscious.

            An ambulance
ferried her away to St John's.

Today she is still unconscious
after the operation last night.

He will understand of course
he cannot visit her       yet.

           His father thinks
that would not be a good idea.

He nods his own head      something is making him
     but he must
why not visit her.

Mrs Hill delivers her answer
 as they curve down from the A120
  past the silage clamp
   sulking under its black tarpaulin
    weighed down with tractor tyres
 through the rip of the ford
beneath the chestnuts with snow congealed on their
 fingertips
   and his mind jars open.

  Squat meringue ambulance
  flash light icy blue flash light
  mud concrete track his mother
  hard black velvet riding hat
  flung aside on a plough crest

  his mother high pillow bank
  yellow hair no hair shaved off
  succulent bruise red green-grey
  eyes shut eyes sunk eye sockets
  octopus oxygen mask clamping

  hiss hiss hiss hiss hiss hiss hisssss
  astronaut capsule open weightless
  bare surface dusty surface pebbly
  a planet no one has visited before.

     *

His grandmother is rotating on the front step at home
 waiting to look after him.

To what.

His grandmother approaching eighty
  frail    deaf    incapable
    utterly perplexed.


    His mother is her daughter.


He reminds himself of this as Mrs Hill disappears
    elated he thinks  like Juliet's mother
      she has done her bit
    and his grandmother offers her cheek
  a soft little rag of crumpled linen
    which irritates him
why    he does not want to think.


Except
  suddenly everything irritates him.


    Everything.


Pink hyacinths his mother propped upright
    with two grey knitting needles
      nevertheless swooning on the hall table.


TV advertising loudly in the sitting room
  to an audience of large empty chairs.


Swish of the dishwasher
  they never use that and anyway
    why at midday.


Most of all his grandmother's dog Janey
  hideous straw-stuffed overstuffed body
    hideous continual barking
  barking    barking    barking

and          come lunchtime
        when it is tethered by his grandmother
            to the leg of the dining-room table
        still barking          barking and lunging
    dragging away the whole table and his plate with it
            as he aims his fork to stab
                cold ham and salad.


                        *


        He pounds upstairs to his bedroom
                and its gloom sanctuary
    curtains permanently drawn even before today
            poster of Soft Machine
            glimmering as if it lived for ever
                    in the incense flicker of altar lights.

He has decided one thing.

        He has decided to anchor
            everything that remains
        in the continual stillness of remembering.

            Therefore
    while his grandmother croons to herself in the spare room
                or Janey maybe
            he visits everywhere in the house
    and examines objects in their places.

The ancient longways-splitting block of grimy soap
in the downstairs washroom used only by his father.

The picture in the hallway of a horse leaping over
a gate with the gate broken but the gate's shadow not.

The tile in the boot room representing the coat of arms
of the Bishop of Chelmsford for reasons he never
   fathomed.

The front door where at sunset with the temperature
   dropping
ice ticks faintly as it tightens on a puddle under the
   hawthorn.

The darkness       not an object
      it might as well be
the darkness back in his room again              the cube
   of safe air
         he thought it was safe
            the darkness now melting in silky strings
                  and droplets
         becoming atoms       prickling atoms
            buzzing and scooting
               colossal buffetings in nature
            but all mute all
               mute
even the infinitely tall gas flame of his mother's scream
               more silent
            than dust settling on moss.


                              *


Every evening now           seven or seven-thirty
      he loiters in his bedroom
and
      when his father's car leaps into the garage
            after his return from hospital
where he has stopped on the way from work

when the chrysanthemum glare of his headlights
     withers against the back wall

     when his father's immaculate black London shoes
stamp across the tarmac to the front door
     at a military pace

he slinks down to the hallway.

He sees his father then
          head and shoulders wavering
through the two glass panels.

My father     he asks himself     my father
          have we met.

     Dark grey London overcoat
               pale grey face
          hair white-grey at the temples
and head bowed under the dome of the outside light.

     Merciless white light
          like the sun of a planet nowhere near to Earth.

His father pauses.

                    His father collects himself.

He pretends to wipe dirt off his shoes.

          Have we met.

Then he squares his shoulders and swoops indoors
     swinging his briefcase and

in a separate plastic bag
a dirty nightie
he extracts with a straight arm
to whizz through to the laundry room
but not before
its chalky talc smell
sweat smell
shit smell
has scribbled its signature
the whole length of the hallway.

*

He is sent back to school.

He finds himself afloat
in a new gravity
thinking about thinking
about living in sadness.

Everyone knows.

Everyone
passes him around and between
like a thousand-year-old
priceless manuscript.

And            despite them all
despite himself
he finds a new occupation.

He becomes Horatio in the spring play.

Not Hamlet.
Horatio.
Goodnight sweet prince.

His mother meanwhile
still floating herself
among the nebulae and gas clouds
of her vast unconsciousness
lands on the moon Pneumonia
where the inhabitants are lotus-eaters
where they dress in mist
where the delectable music
of waterfalls plays continuously
where she is welcomed with murmurs of affection
with kisses
where everyone who lives there
begs her to stay
and everyone looking on
from the far horizon of her hospital bedside
begs her to leave
himself included
when he is allowed to stand there
for the first time
which he understands
will probably be the last time

while his understudy takes over Horatio.

*

Nobody has told him
his mother has become epileptic.

But he sees for himself
when his mother has hauled herself back towards Earth
and his father allows him to visit
alone this time.

He tramps
an eternity of grey linoleum
with a high polish
hard-looking
but surprisingly cushiony underfoot
left     right     straight
left     right     straight
straight     straight     straight     straight
from the front door of St John's
to her ward in a Victorian block
squeezed between the incinerator and a laundry room
as a temporary solution to overcrowding
a hundred years ago.

He steels himself for a long look
at what he has so far only glimpsed
through a cordon of doctors and equipment.

For her shaved head with the stubble
no longer summery fair.

For the orange and red bruise on her temple
maturing to a dead colour
moleskin     trapped     dusty.

For the oxygen tank chipped silver
like treasure salvaged from a wreck.

For her face
        her chin-sag shark face
gaga          mouth hinged with saliva.

But when he arrives round the last corner
                past the nurses' station
into the long ward
                he sees none of this.

There is      his eyes panic
        there is her bed with her
                is this
with her curtain drawn

        with her floor-length pale blue cotton curtain
                twitching and bulging
and black wires          pulleys
        when he pokes his head through the slit

is this
                yes but pinned down      why
in a scrum
        why
                pinned down with four nurses
five
                and a doctor he must be
white coat
        biro scars above the breast pocket
                all of them trying
trying their utmost to
        weigh her down while her body refuses
                while her whole body leaps
like a trout dying in fresh air
                arching clear of the bed

slamming down
    devilish yellow bubbles now in her mouth
        lungfroth
feet dancing
    hands      smothering something
     or strangling


and
      the one in charge
    stethoscope round his neck
       red face
black-frame glasses knocked off his nose almost
   half twisting round without releasing his weight
not for a second
   staring him straight between the eyes
     bellowing

NOT NOW.


          *


  Grief
    too little a word
      no spring-lock inside it
primed
    to snap back to its opposite
  the second her eyes open    again.

  Sorrow    the same.

   Rage    the same.

Limbo then    limbo
   and better accept it.

Limbo.

     Better stretch out an idea
of life itself permanently stretched out
          touching its Michelangelo fingertips     just
against the outstretched fingers of death
     and vice versa.


                              *


In this way
          grief becomes
                         the strange contentment
          of living in suffering
                         without the possibility
of such unhappiness
                    in whatever else
                         remains of life.

Grief
                    even providing a peculiar pleasure
                         sometimes
          like the buzz a mind feels
when a tongue
                    slides over a painful tooth.

Grief     whispering
                    he will be content
          to live in a mirror-bright shining steel universe
               that can never be altered.


                              *

For three years the heat and dampness of her hand
          shit stink
                    sweat stink
                              talcum sweetness
and equally that gargoyle stare
     or her eyelids
               tissue paper
     minuscule knotty purple veins
          fluttering     about to open
                    never opening
only a fish dream
          rising to the surface
                    to sip the light.


     For three years her beautiful thinness
                    bloating into a big belly
          a flagon
pumped with drugs through a murky tube
     darting into the crook of her elbow
          also this other tube
                    clear white
     into a hole in her throat
          through a metal ring
     that will not stop reminding him
of a washer on the pipe below the kitchen sink
          now they have taken her oxygen mask away.


For three years her palm skin and foot skin
     hardening into flawless alabaster

          the stifling hospital heat
sandpaper really

or the charcoal hands of the ward clock
            polishing her
whenever his back turns.

            And all the while nurses
        squeaking on their deep black rubber soles
            or nurses speaking very loudly
        checking her pulse
            honestly shouting
with never a reply
        never a word from her
not for his father        not for him
            gripping her hand
        absorbing the heat and dampness
                        which gave him life.


                        *


Then his mother opens her eyes.

        She looks
and the first thing she sees is somebody else's voice
        abandoned on the stony surface of the world
            she is now leaving.

        She picks it up
            and keeps on leaving.

She tries it out
        this battered trumpet
                these complex throat fingerings.

No.

The voice is not hers.

She does not recognise it.

Nobody does
in this new world
                she means old
    where she is opening her rusty mouth.

It is a husky monotone bass.

A throat wheeze.

A cobwebbed twilit whisper.

But it will do.

It is good enough to blow strange sounds through.

To ask     in so many words
        what happened
                what happened.
Can I come home now.

*

He sits with her every day
    in the evenings his father.

It is their new order.

She speaks to him
        questions him rather
with googly eyes and between sleep-falls
        of disastrous depth and weight.

When he questions her
        her face mystifies.

She remembers light years away
        in miniature
        in a splintering dream tunnel
how he stretched towards her.

Or was that a moment ago
        and no one she knows.

One day he is an infant
        the next he becomes
                the same age as himself.

One day he seizes her attention
        the next his voice signal
                witters into infinite space.

He sits with her every day
        in the evenings his father.

*

A priest arrives
        someone his father knows
to conduct the service of the Laying on of Hands.

Behind the blue curtain drawn round his mother's bed
        with as much silence as possible
                in a ward at visiting time
                    which is to say
with continual squawks        laughter        sobbing
        soft stream-murmurs of chat
chair scraping
        and thrashing in the curtains

                this priest steps forward.

He turns out to be an ordinary man in a suit
        and beneath the dog collar
            a black clerical shirt
        shiny with the impression
            of eternal washings and ironings
and a startling cream and yellow brocaded stole
            he whisks out of nowhere
then drapes around his neck.

He stoops
        and stares with his eyes shut.

He magics a prayer book
        and opens it with both hands
            cradling the floppy crocodile cover.

He murmurs
        as quickly as possible
                a silver stream tinkling over silver stones
embarrassed perhaps
            or is that devout.

And his mother

    he brings himself to look
just about
    at her blazing naked split-openness

      his mother lifts her face
  and her skin tightens
    her skin shines
unearthly subcutaneous candle wax light
    as she devotes herself
      to the difficult work
  of concentrating extremely hard
on making her wish come true.

His father meanwhile
    at the foot of the bed
  clasping his hands together at waist height
and forgetting to hide
    as he usually does
  the forefinger he squashed
    in a deckchair as a child
his father bows his head
    to hide his wet eyes
and tears in the creases beneath his eyes
  and whatever he thinks.

For his own part
    he watches
      still.

He sees    at the appointed moment
    the priest lay aside his prayer book
rest his right hand

                    no press          press his right hand
        no both hands          left piled on right
liver-spotted
        hard onto his mother's forehead
            which burns under the weight
                        and ask God
        to enter her.

Lazarus he thinks
    in the second before
                this really is          more than ever
                intensely embarrassing
    in the second before
                this intense embarrassment
                might be an intervention
                as likely as anything
                to kick-start his mother's rigid body
                a body already dead
                before the mind has left it
                and the heart stops

in other words not.

                        *

He wheels his mother's stretcher
        out from her ward to a corner of the hospital garden
summer grass yellowish between robust clover clumps
        and they sit quietly together
            as mother and son.

Their talk swerves          they like that
        their talk exists again now          and it swerves

but what holds him
        what he cannot avoid coming back to
is the hospital boiler in the shed opposite

        a shed with the wall facing them replaced
            by a single large sheet of glass
to expose the boiler inside.

A boiler                beautiful in its way
        painted valuable silver
                the deep-chested central drum
                dozens of tubes
                offshoots
                returns
                pipes
                drains
                eruptions
all of them shimmering
                the faces on dials
the luxurious flanks
                the dangling and twining arms

        all of them shining like the entrails of a body
housed and cherished outside that body
                and with no ceremony

as discreetly as possible in fact

            in a backwater garden
where no one in the course of a whole long afternoon
        comes to do so much
                as open a stopcock        or read a gauge
                    or polish a drum

simply pursuing its business

        hissing sometimes
emitting occasional clicks and whirrs
      yawning extravagantly

pursuing its business while he and his mother
          meander this way and that
    this way and that in their talk together

       until the light fades

and shadows crawl out of the black grass
      to consume them

       and dew falls

and he has no choice     except to wheel his mother back
      and leave her at her place on the ward.

            *

On Sunday mornings he and his father
      collect his mother
in the Ford Transit christened Billy
      ducking and rolling on the Chelmsford road.

     It is hilarious
terrifying he should say.

No one outside the van could possibly know
    how precarious she is    his mother
      how brittle      how eminently
         smashable

tethered by a flimsy seat belt
      a joke
      in the long shiny-floored metal back of the van
      where         if they braked suddenly

         she would rocket forward
      feet first
      through the shattering windscreen
her brokenness everywhere
         breaking.

    The thought of it keeps them desperate
for the emptiness to stretch
      and last
         all the way home
            with no interruption

      soft fawn club-headed grasses
         curtseying at the curbside

      tyres burbling on sweetly

no interruptions
    except sunlight and tree shadow
      pouncing through the windows

and all the green traffic lights agreeing to let them pass

until they swing off the A120

      the White Hart
      in its childish hollow
      there to the right
      red tile roof

gravel car park
still exactly the same

and slow down through the village
checking the church tower as per
knapped flints flashing their glossy hearts
and bright chalk rims and seams

the village shop Tea Rooms
the old Red Lion    now Rufus Leo a house
always worth a smile

pass the tonsure of the new golf course

and so reach the turning circle
the whispery tarmac outside the front door

and stop

in the blunt shade of the empty extension
built at great cost
where the nurse never
where his mother never

and unload his mother onto the van's tail-lift
squealing under her weight
engine grudging
but up to the job just

while a breeze across the ponies' field frisking
the chestnut tree
the tree with the downward-swooping branch
and patch of shiny bark
where Serenade scratches her back

while a breeze
        flaps away the talcum smell
                nearly

    and he and his father
            inch            squeeze
fiddle his mother's stretcher
        through the front door just
            very tight
                breathe in
they say it every time
                breathe in
    to the hallway and then with a lah-di-dah
make a laugh of it
                four-point turn
            enter the sitting room

park her by the fireside
        busily shuffle up a side table
                set her orange juice there
her pill-bottle battalion

            then                whoosh
                deflate on the sofa
and prepare to talk.


                        *


    He conducts an experiment.

Leaving at the end of visiting hour
    he hammers with his heels
            on the exploding-flower-head carpet tiles

of the corridor to the car park
and sees their blooms
shrivel a little
under the assault of his weight.

He makes as much racket as he decently can
clearing his throat
calling goodbye to the nurses
whistling a merry tune
so his mother will think him gone.

Then he tiptoes back
and peeps round the doorframe.

He sees
which he expects and dreads equally
her head sunk down
on her wafery breastbone.

He sees her eyes
not shut      her eyes blank
blind blue discs
like a statue staring.

He sees her
not herself.

Not present in herself.

He sees her willing herself
to drop through
the detestably tough skin of the world.

*

With no warning

after an arithmetic of years
        he has no reason to think
            are about to become the final amount

pneumonia visits his mother again.

        Pneumonia is a sly one he knows that.

                Pneumonia introduces itself
            as his mother's old friend.

It slips in at her mouth
        when none of the doctors are looking
and curls up inside her
        comfortable as a pussycat dozing.

Then it wakes up and he hears it.

            The growling catarrh.

But his mother.

When he looks into her eyes
        nothing looks back at him.

    She has already heard the delicious promises
            and fallen for them
                why not
            after a very long time.

She has already seen the radiant centre of the world
        where she is free to rise again
            exactly as needed.

As for him
     he thinks he understands completely.

He thinks for the time being
     there is nothing more he can say.

          *       *       *

He remembers            at his mother's funeral

while he is watching his father at her graveside
        his father with smears of Essex clay
            yellowing the heels of his highly polished shoes

his mother telling him
        when his father was a child himself
daydreaming in his bedroom one white afternoon
        he hooked his feet underneath his metal bed rail
            rested his elbows on his knees
                cupped his chin in his hands
so that when his feet slipped and his hands shot upwards
                snapping his mouth shut
            he bit off the tip of his tongue.

What else could he do
                he remembers his mother continuing
        what else could he then do but spit it out
            and carry it carefully downstairs
        to his own mother in the kitchen
                and explain what had happened.

And what else could she do
        but drive to the doctor and ask him
                to sew it on again.

        To save the tongue and make it good as new.

# PART TWO

Since they buried his mother
his father has moved       two hundred yards
and gone to ground himself
in the humid labyrinth fox-earth of a farm cottage
defended by beech hedge fortifications.

He has retired from human friendships
and grown close
to television.

He has poled himself with his ashplant
thumb cocked in the polished cleft
through every conceivable weather
most tellingly rain
to the churchyard and bowed his head
with the same bafflement at her grave
as the empty grass gap waiting beside it.

In this way thirty years have passed
twenty-eight to be precise
and now his patience has been rewarded.

His father has eaten his breakfast
of one soft-boiled egg and white toast soldiers
balanced a mug of tea into his study
and begun what he has to say.

*

In the bedroom of a house in north London
    he is dressing after a shower
        watching as it happens
            dreaming really
    how January daylight gaining strength
        seems to flex

    to roll in subtle almost-invisible waves
        between the lime tree branches
black lime tree branches spotted with white fungus
        latticing his window.

When the telephone rings
        the definite note in his father's voice
            takes him aback.

Bone cancer          his father announces
    shouting softly into the receiver
        poised a good three inches
            away from his mouth.

It is for him a confident start
    but leads nowhere.

A moment later his father has braked hard
    and peers
                teeteringly
        over the cliff edge of his own news.

In the pause
    in the ethereal
            crackling
                vertiginous
        air corridor that opens between them

he imagines his father
        like a soldier on point
whose duty is to reconnoitre
    hostile territory ahead.

He pictures him
    frowning over his desktop
        cleared for battle except
            there is still the question
    of his violated pink blotter
            with its cryptic mirror writing.

Over the front lawn
    crew-cut to a bristling softness.

Over the clenched metallic stubs of rose bushes
    in two symmetrical beds.

Over the beech hedge
    wintering as scraps
        of mysteriously blank brown paper litter
        skewered on twigs.

Over the lane
    where car tyres have battered a loaf
        of green horse dung into the gravel.

Over the stubble field and ragtag crows
    picking through the remains
        of a dead flint giant.

Until he arrives at good cover
    the horizon-wood
        the Ashground

where he tries to avoid remembering
thousands of bluebell bulbs
hoarding their extravagant and ravishing colour tide
under a camouflage of wet leaves.


*


On the train
immediately his father is allowed visitors
the caverns of Liverpool Street
the brilliant moss ledges and lumps
lighting the cindery brickwork
might as well not exist.

Fenchurch and Stratford        Witham and Shenfield.

Then the draggle and widening light
above childhood flatlands
that still bewitch him
with their marvellous corals
and Elvis-quiffed fish
invisible to everyone except himself.

In the surprise of this haste
he wonders under his breath
could it be ending now
this eternal interval with his father
this lifetime of silence.

Throttled
that would be one word
for both of them as bad as each other.

Choked      he admits
by their spitting resemblance
          their
   actually rather relieving
      violent differences of opinion.

At the very idea
      a sensation like sea water
seeping through dry sand
         consumes him.

He stares off
      through the quivering carriage window.

He dreams up
      a superbly powerful blade
   say the scimitar
      Boudicca forged onto her chariot wheel
hacking down perfectly easily
     without the least tremor of resistance
         every Roman soldier track-side telegraph pole

   one-at-a-time
      one-at-a-time
         one-at-a-time
           one-at-a-time

as his train sways woozily forward
    and by magic escapes
      the snake-mess of wires
and failed conversations
      seething in his wake.

*

His eagerness flabbergasts him
        considering he cannot decide yet
            exactly why it exists.

It even survives
            in fact it loves and guzzles
the sweaty air cocktail that envelops him
            the second he revolves
        into the spinning lobby of St John's.

St John's the same
        where they whisked her in
from the midwinter rush-hour hullabaloo
                and Christmas tinsel
        drooping in shop fronts

    then re-dressed her
in washed-out hospital greens
            acquainting themselves in the process
                with her blossoming wound
            her mouth
hanging not quite
                        dead already.


                    *


He stops himself there        this time.

He concentrates instead on his father
        launching himself
            into the old corridor maze
                cautiously for the first few steps
        then allowing a sudden and rapid sweep forward

this way
      this way          this way
that way
        this way

     afloat on the swirling blue linoleum
he half remembers

    taking in        sort of
hotspots where gull-nurses
        gaggle over a titbit

   four five six
        rigid sour yellow plastic doors

    blurred bed-row glimpses

  dozens at least dozens
       of visitors crouched over listening
   or offering

     a cubbyhole for Plant

a clichéd gurney
   rattling its white-as-a-sheet patient
     hell for leather
        and a doctor in hot pursuit

before idling into a backwater
     slowed
       like debris ushered aside from a flood rush
   to inspect
      whether he likes it or not

a long white art gallery wall
    Yorkshire terrier     cottage garden     tabby
    Ravello    onions    sunset

before
    finally
        delivering him.


          *


Ah
    but he has caught his father at a bad moment.

His father    in a chair at his own bedside
    is decked in a stylish
        but sadly only knee-length
    dark-green paisley dressing gown
peculiarly like his own
       and bowed forward with his back turned
          head to head with a doctor
       who has questions he must answer.

He tiptoes closer
    so far still invisible
        to his father at any rate.

The doctor    half his age
          flustered
    flicks him a look
through heavy black-frame Eric Morecambe glasses

      realises
        this must be a son

nods fractionally
                    and continues.

Your work            he asks his father.

        His father cannot remember.

Your middle name.

        His father cannot.

Your birthday.

        His father cannot.

Your regiment.

        His father cannot.

At which point
        he slinks forward
                until his father glimpses him
        in the fish-bowl curve of one lowered eye
turns full face
                    and smiles.

        His father knows one thing then.

And another
                it turns out.

Who is prime minister
        the doctor asks.

BLAIR

     his father spits it out
       as far as possible

BLAIR.


         *


When it is quiet again

      when they are settled
among the murmurings that pass for quiet
         in a twelve-bed ward at visiting time

he feels himself weightless and flying
     on the thermal of what he might call
         his own kindness.

But no.

    It is not kindness.

It cannot be kindness since
     it is not aware of itself.

       It simply exists.

He is a son and
     this is his father     and
       questions at least
are finally possible between them.

To prove it he asks his father
what
has he
really
forgotten.

His father raises an eyebrow
and steers his attention off
through the wide end-window of the ward
to contemplate a red brick water tower
that happens to glower over the hospital hinterland
while scratching idly with his right hand
black beetle therapy scabs on his left arm.

See those pigeons.

He sees them
regular as a posting of sentries
around the battlement of the water tower.

More than this
his father will not say.

*

Next day
which is the first day
of their new existence together
he is still in the trance
of this new gift he was born with.

He exerts himself with no effort
to engage his father's mind.

He drags forward the computer screen
        on its nifty retractable arm
                until it hovers close to his father's chest
        and explains the internet.

His father will not believe
        such a thing is humanly possible.

                You
                mean
                the
                whole
                world.

He shows photographs of his children
        and a vaporous paraffin flame
trims in his father's eyes
        then flops in a cross-breeze.

He dredges and displays
        scenes from his childhood mothering dream flow
but his father was seldom there
        and will not pretend to remember.

He pulls up a different screen
                a talk-screen
        of their rare and valuable excursion
their trip in June 2004
        through the lanes of Normandy
                where his father fought after D-Day.

        Here for a moment
they do sit down together
        with sun toasting their backs

among outrageously large and bright yellow buttercups
in the very field where Colonel Gosling
that would be Mike Gosling
i/c a half-track
came face to face with a Panzer
and

but his father forgets

he presses refresh

but his father

he presses refresh

but his father.

*

Next day and the next
when he turns the corner into his father's ward
and his father now bed-bound
rolls his marble head
to see who          to see what
new interruption
might be approaching
and smiles a child's innocent and complete smile
of recognition and relief
he feels himself a son
as never before.

Airless hospital air
composed of laborious efforts to breathe
continues to bubble under his wings.

Next day and the next
      it raises him off the clinging ground
    the clay that detains him.

He skims
    the treacherous white water linoleum
        pathway approach.

He scans the ward
      like an angel scouting the empyrean
        and halts at a vantage point
where the complete panorama of the world is visible
      and discovers it consists of nothing
    except his father here and now.

He dream-steps and descends
      to his father's blue plastic bedside chair.

He leans close to his father
      like a man in a lighted room
        pressing his face to a window
to make the outside darkness see-through
      in the hood of his own head shadow.

Despite the gigantic
    giddying well-shaft drop
      he sees himself clearly in the depths
craning up to the moon of his own face
      and his mother
    a smear of bridal white.

*

In the light of this
        the chair beside his father's bed
        the snub blue plastic bucket chair
with eminently breakable hollow black metal legs
        has become his one
            right place on Earth.

        Besides which
his father has decided enough is enough
        and crept      rolled
            crept      rolled
dragged himself by minute degrees
        and titanic effort
            across the interminable surface of his ice sheet
to reach the furthest coast of his bed.

        He has turned his back.

        He has confined himself to the window eye
shining in the head of the ward.

When he studies it himself
        adrift
in the almost invisible light current
        he sees as his father sees
        pigeons now and again
            slide off their water tower lookout post
                keep a precise formation
over rows of glittering dolphins
            ploughing the hospital car park
then by consent
        return as they were.

*

Everyone without saying a word agrees

and St John's finds him a bungalow hospice room
      closer to home
           with     as it happens
               a flowering pink cherry
entirely filling the window frame.

And indeed
      the colour overwhelms them both

                  father
           and son

flooding them equally with its blood pulse
          heat illusion
canopy          and soak-through
    while the warm air they breathe together
 sways in a sea swell
        and the breeze tousles.

Not that his father has anything to say about it.

The task of breathing
      now requires his complete attention

        and to address it

he has squared his shoulders
      and drawn himself up to attention
under the large and loose Aertex squares
     of a blue ventilated baby blanket.

      This discipline by his father
this precision

mesmerises him.

There is nothing
    he wants to hear more
        than the silence of his father's tongue

           not to mention this other
              new and ancient language
    lip sounds
throat sounds
    lung sounds
           guts.

Whole hours pass
    while he is perfectly content
to trace the blurred body contours that begot him
        the shapely legs that were good for dancing
           the well-proportioned chest
        concealing the silent heart.

He admires the long arms and nervous hands
    the jumpy hands
        that gave his father's heart away
that shook        that trembled
    that felt and showed the threat
        of every action the world demanded
           down to and including
    deadheading the roses.

He examines
    the sound-asleep hollowing face
        dreaming on its pillow bank

    and discovers it more and more nearly
        resembles his own face.

Until with no warning
no swallow          no cough
        no stir of a nervous hand

his father opens his blue eyes
            their colour astoundingly
                faded to pale cement grey
fixes him and whispers

        never be blackmailed.

                        *

        His invincible father.

When he leaves
        he slips clean
            through the washstand mirror.

        His invincible father.

                        *

The flint village church
    where his father's coffin lies
        all service long
            in a pool of warm gules
        cast by the April sun
    through the fair breast of a window saint
the church
    blackmails the congregation.

The sexton's spade in the churchyard
       which has removed the surface grass
              in delicately snarling curls
and opened the Essex clay
              to a depth of six feet
       exposing black root-wires scrabbling for a hold
the spade
       blackmails the earth.

The priest with his swirling language of dust
       who is the first to throw       timidly
              a clutch of earth onto the far-down coffin lid
       then beckons him forward to do the same
              which he does but kneeling
                     to make the fall
                     and thud less dreadful
the priest
       blackmails the grave.

He backing away from the grave eyeing the sexton
       who himself eyes these proceedings
from the dark flame of an ancient yew tree
       and trampling       almost
              on the grave of his mother
he
       blackmails himself.

His mother who has waited thirty years
       for her husband to climb into the bed beside her
       and whose name has faced into the rain so long
its letters are now slivers of grey moss
his mother
       blackmails everyone.

None of which
            he thinks
      as he stumps up the incline of the village street
   towards the wake in the garden of his father's cottage
                  makes the slightest sense
               and will never.

PART THREE

After forty years Juliet emails him.

Can they meet.

He reads her message again      and again
    counts.

Forty years.

Since their first    last    date
        and lamplight
sweating on those oak panels in her spare bedroom
    magnolia leaves
        pat-patting a leaded window.

Four zero.

Since her slithering black hair
        creamy swimmer's shoulders
            her big soft wide
words still fail him
        mouth.

*

He delays answering

        a minute
    is hardly decent.

Very well another
        drumming his fingers
then                                clickety-click at the gallop

    and                        send.


                          *


St Pancras station        the Booking Office Bar
        which is her idea.

He arrives early like a fool
        giddy a bit
            thanks to his head-back stare
                at the barrel vault roof
and sunset's lilacs and charcoals
            staining the many-coloured glass.

        Or are they ghosts of the steam age?

At any rate
        he expects to kill time
        inspecting John Betjeman
            coming or going or both
                in his flapping bronze mac
                    trainspotting the Eurostar
                flyblown chisel-face of the future.


                          *


        But Juliet is before him.

It must be          Juliet
          trailing in one hand her overnight wheelie bag
                    the other
          clamped to a mobile and why not
          husband probably
                    in Paris already or wherever.

And why not.

          Except his disappointment exists
                    and is frankly
scandalous even to him.


                              *


Juliet     he remembers now
                              she told him
          is wearing dark glasses.

          Very big          black-framed
                              curved
          very dark dark glasses
masking her face
                    as far as possible.

          That is all he has time for.

          Bye     she says.
                    That is her first word.

To the phone naturally.

Bye.

As her wheels trundle to a halt.

As he imagines himself replying
        when in fact he is silent
            and staring.

Not the white hand
        smuggling her mobile into the slit
            of a navy overcoat pocket.

Not the beautiful black bob
        grey at the roots.

Not the mouth
            thinned under its lipstick twirl
        think of the millions of breaths
            the words
smoking over her lips
            think of feet wearing down a threshold.

He is staring
        at scars on her face.

    Scars dicing into her lips
            little hairline fractures
                    glaze cracks
            fissures and faults
not faults no
            scars.

What happened.

    These are his first words
            after forty years.

What happened.

\*

  Juliet's hair shakes
blooms in a bridling pony-toss
   then soothes
    and fits neatly again.

Therefore
  he pretends he has seen nothing
   and with a bluff enthusiasm
    which for all she knows
  is now his natural everyday manner
   steers her into the bar of the Booking Office
and round to a
   bloody miracle
    empty corner table
without another word spoken.

\*

In their background
  departure times and destinations
   trudge through watery echoes.

In their immediate vicinity
  high-gloss woodwork  new olde England
   horse-brasses
    and everyone taking a breather.

  He follows suit.

He orders house white
        and the waitress who understands
                speed is the essence
    rattles it down
            in a profoundly nervous silvery ice bucket.


                        *


Juliet meanwhile
            eases her dark glasses
        a fraction along her nose
            and rests them on a pale skin-ridge
the main scar there
        to hide it.

She has no time to waste
        and without the least flourish or sidestep
                delivers a boiled-down
                        recitative
namely     her life since last they met
                    and parted.

        Au pair                  marriage
        two children                girls
        living in                freelance
        films     documentaries mostly.


                        *


He shuffles his glass on the tabletop
            creased apparently
            with ghostly cloth wipes

and cannot prevent himself
　　still looking
　　　　when he thinks she is not looking.

　　At her hair sweetly hooked behind one ear.

At her jittery ear stud on its plump little flesh-cushion.

　　At her white throat　　　　very white throat
　　　　swelling when she swallows
in the shadowy collar V
　　　　　　of her expensive black silk shirt.

At her surprising　　　　forgotten
　　　　blunt-tipped　　almost square-ended fingers
　　nails unpainted　　milky suns
　　　rising from the cuticle.


　　　　　　　　　　*


Then his turn　　　he thinks.

　　But that is not what she came for.

　　She stalls him.

　　　She slips off her dark glasses
　　　　　　and shows him her white face
naked.


　　　　　　　　　　*

If she told him a wild cat
            launching out of a pine forest

if she told him a lightning strike

            a firework

an alleyway bottle-end lunge

        if she told him a particularly sharp idea
            an idea like a star birthing
                the most brilliant idea imaginable
had shattered out of her brain
                        through her left cheek
                engulfed her left eye
and scorched her mouth

            he would believe her.

But          a company car
        the M40 late at night
                    darkness      rain
                and roly-poly down the embankment
outside High Wycombe

                    High
        Wycombe

    which Juliet offers
                without him asking
he cannot accept
            and must.

                    *

No sooner
        the wet tarmac rubber smear
            the barrier can-opened
        the mud gouge      the grass rip
the steaming hush and blue dashboard glow

        than his mother of course.

    His mother in her own seamless flash footage
head shaved gingery bare
                tiger-slash operation scar
    eyes pulpy      bruise-mashed
        oxygen      tank      tube      mask
                oxygen itself
pressing a skeletal finger to pursed lips

        sssssssssshhhhhhhhh.

                *


Juliet fills her glass          his glass
        but for him enough.

            Enough.

If he had come with a plan.

    If he had ever          and he had
                he sees that now
    in corn-yellow soft focus.

If he had ever imagined they might.

        Then                shame on him.

Shame on him and
　　　　why not just creep away immediately
　　　with his tail and whatever else
　　　　tucked between his legs.


　　　　　　*


Which Juliet has no time for.

　　She is watching the clock.

　　　　She is insisting her point is not
　　only the accident　　　her point
　　　is after the accident
　　　　　she lay unconscious three days.


　　　　　　*


Midwinter fields
　　　　no footprint
　　among flint bones
　　　　and bristly Essex clay lumps
no shadow
　　　the seething snow surface
　　　　　opening
　　and closing its lacy arms.


　　　　　　*


Unconscious Juliet continues
　　　　then awake but not

awake-awake          not
          herself.


     More like a radio dial twiddling
picking on day one
          a French signal
     and her voice speaking only French
          on day two
                    her voice in English
                              with a French accent
          on day three normal
her everyday voice
          beaming back to her
     from the spangling gas-warps
                    of infinite deep brain space.


                    *


A waitress at the table adjacent
     clears cutlery like glittery fish in a handful.

He meanwhile
          sponges up what he hears.

     He wrings out Juliet's languages
               and squeezes them into his own language
     storing them
          along with the car wreck
     the rain the rain the rain          the headlights
          stubbed in embankment plough.

Although     as the debris
          the confetti windscreen glass
               the smashed boxer's face fender

the car radio
        churning its exciting trash regardless
            and        in the midst of it all
Juliet's silence
        her scarred face        her unconsciousness


        as the combined weight of this
    groans
    creaks
    scrapes
    sinks
    settles
        and enters his consciousness


he reminds himself
        Juliet is not his punishment.


            Not if he chooses.


                        *


At which point
        she arrives at the point
            that brought her here in the first place.

She tells him        at last and suddenly
        she can remember nothing
            of her life before the accident.

She explains
        having forgotten everything herself
    her sister remembered
            she knew him once.

She asks him
     what passed      please
       between them.

She is in his hands
       she says.

*

He straightens
       to meet Juliet's eye.

To enter her eye and drop
     through liquid green-flecked chestnut brown
    into the dead centre.

Which is prepared to believe him.

     Which is waste land.

       A cat look
  I know you     do I know you
     remind me.

*

He deliberates.

   He weighs her featherweight weight.

And he lets her go.

He lets her life go
        and Juliet in their time remaining
   bare faced        dressed in her wounds
            leans forward
        to catch what he has to say.